To Ms. Bradley's 5th grade class —

Revise! Revise! Revise!

Mark D.

Books in the Series:

Origami Oohs & Aahs for Writing Students
6 Tricks to Student PERSUASIVE Writing Success
Kids Webmastering with HTML
6 Tricks to Student DESCRIPTIVE Writing Success
6 Tricks to Student EXPOSITORY Writing Success

6 Tricks to Student STORY Writing Success

An Easy Guide for Students, Teachers & Parents

Mark Diamond

creator of
Writing to Command Attention!™ Workshops

illustrations by Jim Gilbert

an Anyone Can Write™ book

An Anyone Can Write Book
published in 2005

Anyone Can Write Books
2890 N. Hills Dr. NE
Atlanta, GA 30305

First Printing 2005

ISBN: 0-9771470-0-2

Illustrations: Jim Gilbert

WITH THANKS TO

Fran, Jamie, Esther, Dorothy, Cheryl, Jay, Elaine, Jim, Paulette, Tracy, Betty, Ralph, Janice, Dr. R, Leland

&

the thousands of test bunnies (students, teachers & parents)

who certify that this method works!

CONTENTS

Why We Won't Write

Simple four-letter word answer:

F - E - A - R

Of what?

Failure

Making Mistakes

Criticism

Our Excuses

"I can't think of anything."

"I'm thinking! I'm thinking!"

"I don't understand the topic."

"My hand hurts."

"Nothing like the topic has ever happened to me."

"We don't have a TV." (if writing topic is TV-related)

"It's too hard!"

"I can't concentrate with all these distractions."

The Solution

The 3 A's of Writing

Attitude

(what we should say to ourselves)

"WE LOVE MISTAKES!"

"We love spelling, grammar and punctuation mistakes!"

"We'll fix the mistakes later!"

"The only mistake is NOT WRITING AT ALL!"

Atmosphere

eliminate distractions

soft lighting

listen to smooth jazz instrumental music

(it covers distracting noise)

Activities

Write about PERSONAL EXPERIENCE topics, like:

performing in front of an audience

a big success or failure, like winning or losing an election

losing someone or something of great importance, like a relative, friend, pet or favorite ring

most embarrassing moment

most memorable consequence or punishment

5 Steps of Writing

Writing is a little like assembling a toy or model.

To do it right, follow the steps outlined in the directions.

But instead of a zillion steps, here are 5:

Writing Step 1

Prewriting

PRE means *before,* so this is all the stuff we do *before* writing:

BRAINSTORMING (think hard without rejecting ideas)
PLANNING (make topic & character decisions)
STORY WEB (list story-related items)

WOW! LINE™ (we'll get there soon)

Writing Step 2

Drafting

1st draft
rough draft
sloppy copy

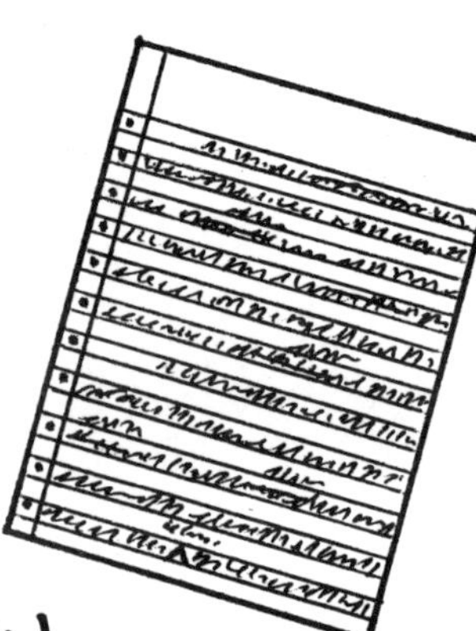

Write quickly and don't worry about mistakes.

Use pencil only.

Write on every 2nd line to leave revising space.

Use complete sentences.

No erasing! (You might want to put something back.)

~~Instead, cross out using one thin line.~~

No balling up paper and starting over! If you don't like something, cross it out. Too much good stuff ends up in the trash can.

Don't sweat it if you're not happy with your 1st draft.

Even professional writers are disappointed with their 1st drafts.

1st drafts are like bones - a skeleton of your story.

We'll add the heart and soul later, in **REVISING.**

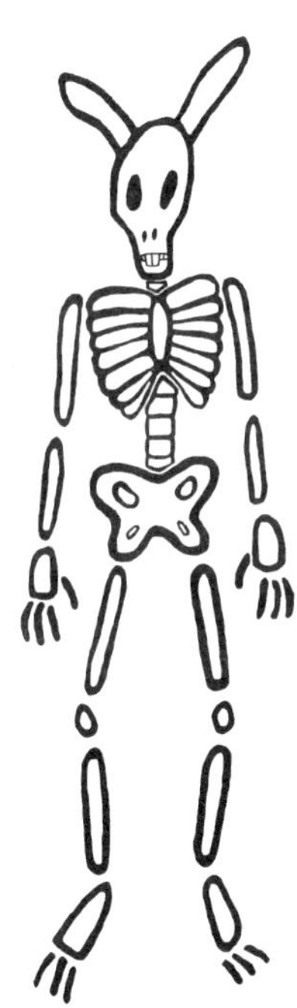

Writing Step 3 Revising (make it great!)

MOST IMPORTANT STEP OF WRITING!

Revising BOOSTS Your Writing

from

GOOD ⟶ GREAT!

add stuff

delete stuff

move stuff

substitute better words

(see Tricks 3, 4 & 5 - pages 48-61)

Writing Step 4

Proofreading

sometimes wrongly called "editing"

CORRECT MISTAKES, like

SPELLING	I spy a dust bunnie.
PUNCTUATION	Look theres a carrot!
GRAMMAR	They was funny bunnies.

Writing Step 5

Publishing

neat sheet
final draft
final copy

COPY IT OVER NEATLY

Use erasable pens for last-minute little changes.

This is NOT the step for making lots of changes or writing new stuff.

Input to your computer! Make a book! Add drawings!

THE
AMAZING
RALPH
THE
WRITING
WIZARD

The 6 Tricks

or

Why does writing have to be so hard?

(and what you can do about it)

~~"It takes years of hard work to become a student story writing success."~~

WRONG!

This is what the old-fashioned, traditional educational publishers want you to believe, so schools will keep spending their precious bucks on big, fat, BORING textbooks THAT DON'T WORK!

Don´t listen to them! There´s an easy way!

RIGHT!

Learn the following 6 Tricks
and achieve student story writing success
in just 3 weeks or less!

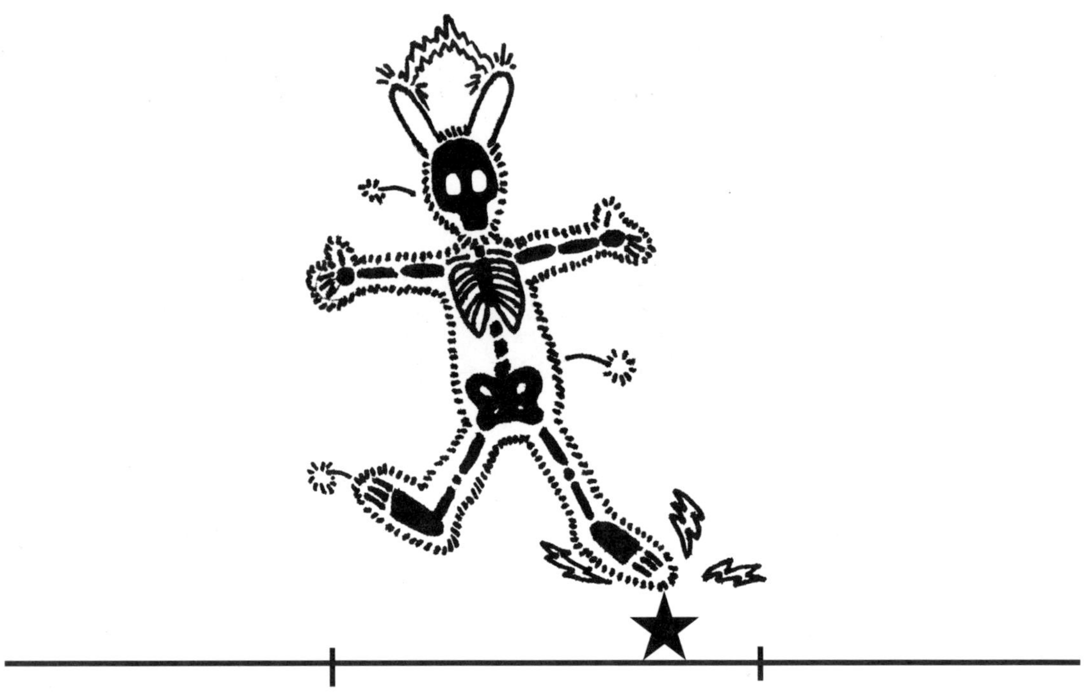

Trick #1

The Wow! Line™

Planning your story's parts

Construction workers cannot build a house without blueprints, can they?

If they tried it, the house would fall apart during a fierce thunderstorm.

Without a
solid story plan,
your story will
fall apart also,
creating
boredom and
confusion
for your reader.

Wow! line to the rescue!

Always make and fill one out **BEFORE** you begin your **SLOPPY COPY** (1st draft).

Draw a horizontal line to represent your story.

beginning	middle	end

Divide it into the 3 parts that EVERY STORY MUST HAVE.

Draw a ★ toward the
END OF THE MIDDLE SECTION.

The ★ is your story's WOW! MOMENT.

When readers read what happens at the ★, they say "WOW!" in their heads.

Every story **MUST HAVE A WOW! MOMENT** (or your story will be boring).

NOW DECIDE!

What is the WOW! MOMENT in your story?

What is the most INTENSE moment?

What moment will make the readers exclaim "WOW!" in their heads?

Jot a note about what happens at the WOW! MOMENT above the ★.

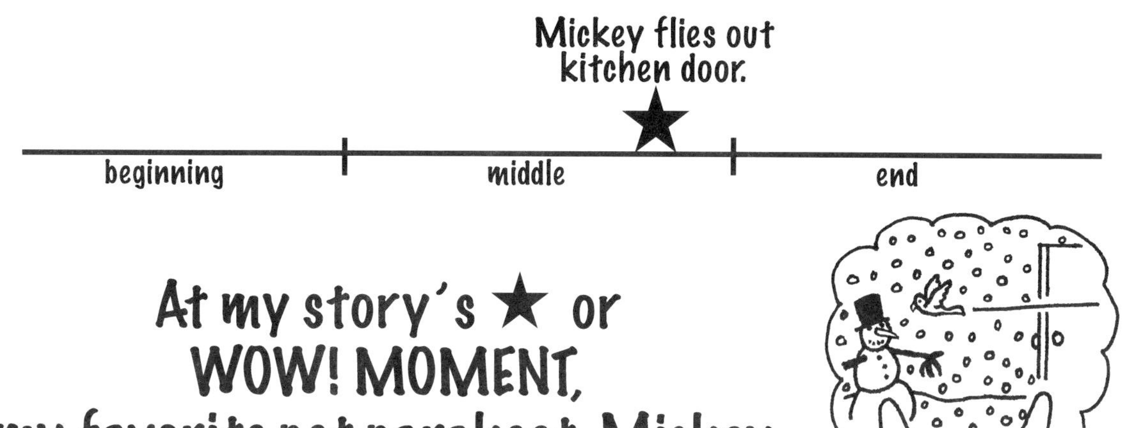

At my story's ★ or
WOW! MOMENT,
my favorite pet parakeet, Mickey,
flies out the kitchen door
into a blizzard.

I can just see my readers thinking, "**WOW!**"

From your ★ or **WOW! MOMENT**,
press **REWIND** in your brain.

Go all the way back to the beginning of your story.

My story's beginning section will be
ALL ABOUT MICKEY & ME -
when I first got him,
describing him & training him.

I'll jot this down at the beginning of my **WOW!** line.

Finally, FAST FORWARD to the end section of your story and jot down what happened AFTER the WOW! MOMENT.

The blueprint of the story is complete. Time to begin the SLOPPY COPY!

Not so fast!

First, we've got to create an attention-getting first sentence, called...

Trick # 2

The LEAD (first sentence)

CATCH YOUR READER'S ATTENTION!

The LEAD does not:

tell what happens at the Wow! Moment
mention the subject or topic
start with "One day," "One night," "One warm and windy Thursday afternoon," "Hi, my name is Tiffany," or "Have you ever...?"

Effective Lead #1

DIALOGUE (someone speaking)

example: "Come downstairs, Derrick," yelled mom.

TIP: If your lead sentence forces a question to pop up in the readers' minds, they'll have to KEEP READING to answer that question.

example: "Come downstairs, Derrick. You're late," yelled mom.

What's the pop-up question in the reader's mind?

RESULT: The reader has to **KEEP READING** to answer that question!

NOW YOU'VE CAUGHT THE READER'S ATTENTION!

Effective Lead #2

SMALL MOVEMENT

example: Allison kicked the can into the stream.

POP-UP QUESTIONS: Who is Allison? Why is she kicking a can into the stream? Where is she?

TIP: Remember that this is NOT the MAIN ACTION, which is usually at the ★

Effective Lead #3

WHAT SOMEONE THINKS or FEELS

example : "I don't want to do this," Jamie thought.
POP-UP QUESTION: What doesn't Jamie want to do?

example: Beads of sweat formed on my forehead.
POP-UP QUESTION: What's wrong?

TO FIND OUT, THE READER MUST KEEP READING!

IN REVIEW:

The LEAD is your story's most important sentence

(whether non-fiction or fiction).

Professional writers **don't** start with "One day..." or "One night..."

WHY SHOULD YOU?

Start noticing the LEAD of every chapter in your chapter books.

9 out of 10 chapters will begin with one of these 3 EFFECTIVE LEADS:

1 DIALOGUE
2 SMALL MOVEMENT
3 WHAT SOMEONE THINKS OR FEELS

CHECK IT OUT, THEN USE THEM!

SLOPPY COPY time!

WRITE YOUR STORY QUICKLY WITHOUT WORRYING ABOUT MISTAKES OR SPECIFIC DETAILS.

Follow TIPS about
Writing Step 2 - Drafting
from page 18

REVISING – make it great!

Trick # 3 Revising Step A

ADD SPECIFIC DETAILS AND DIALOGUE TO THE ★ PART

(detail: a small piece of information or description)

LOCATE the **WOW! MOMENT** in your Sloppy Copy.
ADD some specific (exact) details to this part.
ADD some dialogue.

If you can't remember exactly what happened or what someone said, **MAKE IT UP!**

Use a ^ to add a few words.
caret (written above the ^)

BEFORE: As Maria slammed the door behind her,
she saw a flash of green shoot toward the clouds.

AFTER: As Maria slammed the door behind her,
she ^ saw a flash of green shoot toward the clouds.
heard the flutter of wings and (inserted at the ^)

But if you need to

ADD MORE THAN A FEW WORDS,

write the extra sentences on
another sheet of paper.

LABEL THE SHEET OF EXTRA SENTENCES WITH A SYMBOL, LIKE ⊛ .

Also, place the ⊛ where the extra sentences go on your Sloppy Copy.

As you find more places to add extra sentences, use other symbols, like ▲ or ☺ or make up your own!

Trick # 4 Revising Step B

ADD UNUSUAL DETAILS AT 1st MENTION OF MAIN CHARACTER or SUBJECT (IN BEGINNING PART)

LOCATE the place in your Sloppy Copy where you first mention your main character or subject.

ADD some unusual or fascinating details about this person, pet, place or object.

Use a caret to add a few words, or extra page with symbols to add several sentences.

BEFORE: Mickey was a parakeet. He was pretty. We had a lot of fun together.

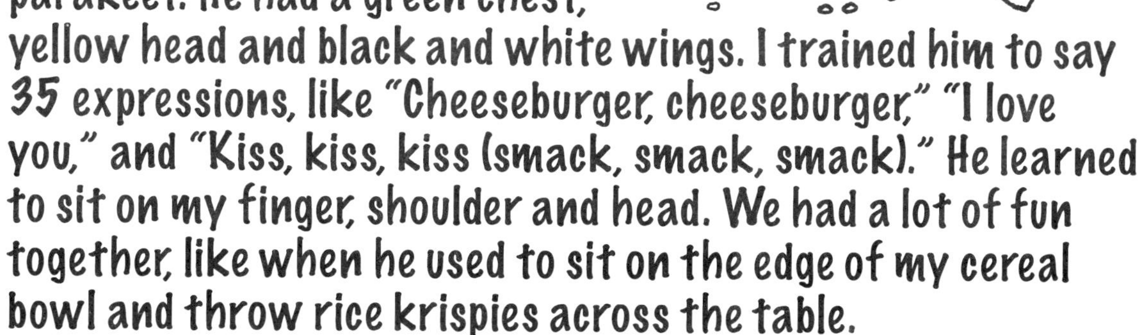

AFTER: Mickey was a fist-sized parakeet. He had a green chest, yellow head and black and white wings. I trained him to say 35 expressions, like "Cheeseburger, cheeseburger," "I love you," and "Kiss, kiss, kiss (smack, smack, smack)." He learned to sit on my finger, shoulder and head. We had a lot of fun together, like when he used to sit on the edge of my cereal bowl and throw rice krispies across the table.

Trick # 5 Revising Step C

SUBSTITUTE SPECIAL WORDS

Our Sloppy Copy is full of common, everyday words, like the words we use when we speak.

Now it's time to make our writing sound special and more mature.

HOW?

... BY REPLACING OUR NORMAL,
COMMON WORDS AND EXPRESSIONS

WITH

PRECISE
VIVIDLY DESCRIPTIVE
UNCOMMON

WORDS and PHRASES

trudged through blizzard
Maria ~~walked over in~~ the ~~snow and ice~~. After she

arrived brushed
~~got there~~, she ~~got~~ the snow and ice off her coat and hat

removing
before ~~taking~~ them ~~off~~. "Want to sit and have some hot

asked
chocolate?" ~~said~~ mom.

replied grabbing nearest
"Mmm, thanks," ~~said~~ Maria, ~~taking~~ the chair ~~close to~~

Meanwhile, rim
the kitchen window. ^ Mickey sat on the ~~edge~~ of my cereal

tossing toward
bowl, ~~throwing~~ rice krispies across the table ~~to~~ Maria.

These word and phrase substitutions make our writing sound more adult and professional.

THEY **BOOST** OUR WRITING FROM

GOOD ⟶ GREAT!

C ⟶ A!

Here's a descriptive word list for further Revising C - SUBSTITUTE SPECIAL WORDS

SAID	LAUGHED	RAN	SAD
called	snickered	hurried	downcast
cried	giggled	raced	depressed
responded	roared	scurried	despondent
demanded	chuckled	dashed	gloomy
asked	chortled	galloped	miserable
stated	crowed	trotted	sorrowful
shouted	guffawed	bolted	unhappy
whispered	cackled	darted	dejected
remarked	howled	sped	forlorn
questioned	tittered	jogged	melancholy
replied	bellowed	sprinted	crestfallen
exclaimed	whooped	rushed	mournful
screamed		scampered	distressed
explained			

MORE SPECIAL WORDS

WALKED	SAW	LIKE	HAPPY
staggered	glimpsed	love	glad
traveled	noticed	admire	jovial
trudged	observed	appreciate	jubilant
strutted	sighted	fancy	joyful
marched	spotted	adore	thrilled
hiked	stared at	idolize	cheerful
shuffled	glanced at	prefer	buoyant
sauntered	eyed	cherish	contented
lumbered	gazed at	care for	pleased
paraded	spied	favor	delighted
ambled	examined	enjoy	ecstatic
strolled	watched	treasure	elated

EVEN MORE SPECIAL WORDS

PRETTY	SMART	GOOD	LITTLE
beautiful	bright	first-rate	teeny
lovely	quick-witted	pleasant	diminutive
gorgeous	intelligent	marvelous	compact
glamorous	clever	delightful	microscopic
attractive	ingenious	superior	petite
elegant	sharp	splendid	wee
cute	brainy	superb	small
exquisite	brilliant	top-notch	tiny
stunning	on-the-ball	terrific	miniscule
handsome	wise	amazing	miniature
striking	knowledgeable	excellent	slight
fair		awesome	minute
appealing		wonderful	itty-bitty

FINAL SPECIAL WORDS (Promise!)

FUNNY	NICE	BIG	ANGRY
amusing	kind	towering	irate
humorous	benevolent	huge	mad
witty	thoughtful	large	perturbed
comical	gracious	great	enraged
hysterical	considerate	gigantic	incensed
sidesplitting	decent	mammoth	sore
hilarious	congenial	enormous	infuriated
laughable	agreeable	tremendous	vexed
silly	courteous	massive	upset
jocular	warm	giant	angered
nonsensical	cordial	colossal	worked up
entertaining	humane	immense	aggravated
riotous	generous	humongous	exasperated
		monumental	annoyed
			furious

THE END
HMMM...

Trick # 6

The CONCLUSION

(Closing, Ending)

NO MORE "THE END"

Fairy tales and books for very young kids finish with

"THE END"

Now we're ready to write endings that

SOUND LIKE ENDINGS,

not like we just stopped!

Reasons our endings sometimes sound like we just stopped:

"I RAN OUT OF TIME."

"I REACHED THE BOTTOM OF MY PAPER."

"I GOT TIRED OF WRITING."

"I COULDN'T THINK OF ANYTHING ELSE TO SAY."

"MY HAND HURT."

HOW'S THIS ENDING FOR A TRUE STORY ABOUT WHEN I WON THE ELECTION FOR CLASS PRESIDENT?

"After dinner, we drove home and I went to sleep."

Not very good, right? Why not?

Try this ending:

"After dinner, we drove home and I went to sleep. All that night, I couldn't stop thinking about the exciting projects I'd be working on as the new class president."

It works, doesn't it? Why?

(Turn the page for the answer.)

THE NEW ENDING WORKS BECAUSE IT IS EITHER

a **thought**
a **feeling**, or
a **lesson learned**

ABOUT THE MAIN TOPIC.

HOW'S THIS ENDING FOR A TRUE STORY ABOUT WHEN MY BEST FRIEND MOVED TO ANOTHER CITY?

"After Chris moved away, I went home and watched TV."

LET'S REVISE IT.

"After Chris moved away, I went home and watched TV, but it felt lonely without my best friend watching with me. I hope we get to see each other again real soon."

SOUND LIKE AN ENDING? YOU BET!

~~When I Lost My Carrots~~

~~The~~ Time I Fell Off My Bike

~~My Favorite Wristwatch~~

~~Our Family Camping Trip~~

~~The Day My Hamster Ran Away~~

~~The Winning Election~~

TITLES...

Never tell, but only hint, at what's to come.

OUR TITLES USUALLY GIVE TOO MUCH INFORMATION. OFTEN, THEY SPOIL THE STORY FOR THE READER BY "GIVING AWAY" THE **WOW! MOMENT.**

Do you like it when your friends tell you what happens in a movie you want to see?

DEFINITELY NOT!

Titles should make the reader WONDER,

"WHAT IS THIS STORY ABOUT?"

How's this title for my story about a family camping trip?

<u>Our Family Camping Trip</u>

THUMBS DOWN!

That title **TELLS**, when it should **HINT**.

TRY THIS ONE: **Mountains & Mosquitoes**

YEP! IT WORKS BECAUSE READERS WON'T UNDERSTAND WHAT IT MEANS UNTIL THEY READ THE STORY.

"Oh, that's why it's called Mountains & Mosquitoes," readers will say.

TIP: Choose a title **AFTER** you write your story!

"The... snow... was... falling... so... hard... I... could... barly..." barly? Hmm, I need to put an "e" after the "r" so it's "barely," not "barly."
"I... could... barely... see..." Oops! I forgot to put a period after "see."
"I... didn't... no..." Uh, oh! I used the wrong "no." It should be "know."
The snow was falling so hard I could barly see I didn't no how I was going to find my parakeet.

Fool-Proof Proofreading™

FACT: Scientific studies prove that
SILENT PROOFREADING DOES NOT WORK.

FACT: Having a partner proofread your story
DOES NOT HELP YOUR PROOFREADING SKILLS.

FACT: Careless proofreading for errors leads the reader to
LOSE RESPECT FOR THE WRITER.

FACT: Proofreading can be as easy as **A, B & C.**

The ABC's of Proofreading

A Proofread in a low voice so your ears can hear mistakes.

B Point to each word with your pencil as you say the word.

C Proofread in slow motion.

Prove It!

Prove to yourself this proofreading plan really works!

Go get one of your 1st drafts now and try it out!

REMEMBER:

REMEMBER:	A	low voice
	B	point
	C	slo-mo

PARAGRAPHING

Don't you hate it when you have to read a bunch of pages without indents? There's just so many... WORDS! Words everywhere, with no break in sight! Whew!

We need some indents so we can catch our breath, don't we?

OK, calm down. INDENTS to the rescue!

INDENTS HELP THE READERS TAKE TINY RESTS WHILE READING, SO THEY DON'T BURN OUT.

But how does the writer figure out where to place these indents?

EASY. MOVE ALONG.

5 Reasons to Make New Paragraphs

1. at the <u>beginning</u>
2. change of <u>idea</u> or <u>topic</u>
3. change of <u>place</u>
4. change of <u>time period</u> (day, week, month, year)
5. change of <u>speaker</u> (even if only one sentence has been spoken)

Use the paragraph sign ¶ to show an indent on your Sloppy Copy before writing your Neat Sheet.

WRONG!

RIGHT!

CLEEB:™ 5 Tips for Super Oral Presentations

Have you ever become bored or sleepy while listening to a writer read a story?

Sometimes the story is fantastic,
but the presentation
makes it sound terrible!

As writers, we need to be impressive presenters to make our stories take flight.

IT TAKES PRACTICE TO MASTER THE FOLLOWING TIPS, BUT IT'S A SKILL YOU'LL USE FOREVER.

Here's the CLEEB method of super oral presentation:

Clear	speak clearly
Loud	speak loudly
Expression	speak with feeling, like TV or movie actors
Eye contact	sometimes look up from you paper to communicate with your eyes
Body movement	no leaning-stand up straight two hands on paper (gesture with one if needed) paper held at chest height

OPENING CLEEB TIPS

BEFORE STARTING TO READ:

get into proper reading position

make eye contact with each audience member from one side of the room to the other side

if you see someone not paying attention, clear your throat to alert them that you are ready to begin

SOMETIMES PRESENTERS RUSH OFF SO FAST THAT THEIR FINAL WORDS ARE LOST. TRY THESE TIPS.

CLOSING CLEEB TIPS

read the closing sentence SLOWLY

use MORE EYE CONTACT during closing

after the closing sentence, PAUSE before moving back to your seat

THESE TIPS IMPART MORE IMPORTANCE TO THE CLOSING, LEAVING YOUR AUDIENCE WITH SOMETHING TO THINK ABOUT.

Now Get Out There and Write!

Don't Be Afraid to Make Mistakes!

The Only Thing You Can Do Wrong is Not Writing At All!

REVISE! REVISE! REVISE!

WRITE!!!
WRITE!!!
WRITE!!!

Meet Mr. D

Known to thousands of students as "Mr. D," Mark presents more than 250 seminars each year for elementary and middle school students, faculty and parents. His *Writing to Command Attention!* writing workshops merge learning with fun, providing lifelong skills in an entertaining package. Mark also has been a creative writing & gifted ed teacher, journalist, rock band manager & sound mixer, photographer and instructional TV director.

E-mail Mr. D at Mark@AnyoneCanWrite.com or visit his website:
www.AnyoneCanWrite.com

Mr. D

ORDER FORM

ORDER ON-LINE: www.AnyoneCanWrite.com

POSTAL ORDERS: (check or PO only)

Anyone Can Write Books
2890 N. Hills Dr. NE
Atlanta, GA 30305
Mark@AnyoneCanWrite.com

Please send me ____ copies of *6 Tricks to Student STORY Writing Success*

1-9 copies @ $14.95 each   10-29 @ $12.95 each   30+ @ $10.00 each

Georgia residents add 7% state sales tax

School ______________________ Tax-Free ID # __________

Name ______________________________________

Address ______________________________________

City ______________ State __________ Zip __________

Phone number ______________________

E-mail address ______________________

SHIPPING: $2.50 single copy; e-mail for multiple-copy shipping costs

Notes

ORDER FORM

ORDER ON-LINE: www.AnyoneCanWrite.com

POSTAL ORDERS: (check or PO only)

Anyone Can Write Books
2890 N. Hills Dr. NE
Atlanta, GA 30305
Mark@AnyoneCanWrite.com

Please send me ____ copies of *6 Tricks to Student STORY Writing Success*

1-9 copies @ $14.95 each 10-29 @ $12.95 each 30+ @ $10.00 each

Georgia residents add 7% state sales tax

School ____________________ Tax-Free ID # __________

Name ______________________________________

Address ______________________________________

City ______________ State __________ Zip __________

Phone number ____________________

E-mail address ____________________

SHIPPING: $2.50 single copy; e-mail for multiple-copy shipping costs

Notes

ORDER FORM

ORDER ON-LINE: **www.AnyoneCanWrite.com**

POSTAL ORDERS: (check or PO only)

Anyone Can Write Books
2890 N. Hills Dr. NE
Atlanta, GA 30305
Mark@AnyoneCanWrite.com

Please send me ____ copies of *6 Tricks to Student STORY Writing Success*

1-9 copies @ $14.95 each   10-29 @ $12.95 each   30+ @ $10.00 each

Georgia residents add 7% state sales tax

School ____________________ Tax-Free ID # __________

Name ____________________________________

Address ____________________________________

City ______________ State __________ Zip __________

Phone number ____________________

E-mail address ____________________

SHIPPING: $2.50 single copy; e-mail for multiple-copy shipping costs